Derrick + Barba!

Your happiness all y___ __ the Joy to life.
is contagious. the key to ___ be.
the Lord is the key ___
Strength. God has prepared
you a special blessing that will
Surprise all — walk into your destiny

Bishop J.L. Parks
6-13-03

Dream Series

Holding On to Your Dreams

*Reaching Your True Potential
in the Will of God*

Bishop J. C. Parks

Noble House
Baltimore, Maryland

Holding On to Your Dreams

Library of Congress
Cataloging-in-Publication Data
ISBN 1-56167-769-8

Library of Congress Card Catalog Number:
2002094686

Published by

8019 Belair Road, Suite 10
Baltimore, Maryland 21236

Manufactured in the United States of America

Contents

"Eye has not seen, nor ear heard, neither have entered into the heart of man, the things which God hath prepared for them that love him. But God hath revealed them unto us by His Spirit; for the Spirit searcheth all things, yea, the deep things of God"

I Corinthians 2: 9-10

To my late mother and father, Tommie and Lela Parks, that encouraged me to never let go of my dreams.

PREFACE

Dear Reader,

I want to help you understand God's way of leading you to the achievement of your destiny. God inspires us with dreams of what we could become. These dreams may seem like simple continual thoughts, or strong desires. However, these thoughts or desires are seed thoughts from God. You should not confuse daydreaming with divine revelation. Dreams are God's way of showing us our predestination. Our challenge is to believe God's revelation of our destiny, despite our struggles.

The story of Joseph is one of many stories found in the book of Genesis. However, I believe that this story contains a key to helping us to achieve and maintain the extraordinary favor of God. This story has radically changed what I expect from God; has increased my understanding of my life's struggles; and how I should see myself in His will. If you can apply the truths contained in this little book, you will see miracles happen on a regular basis on your way to achieving your dreams.

I hope that your each and every dream becomes a reality; press down, shaken together, and running over.

Dreams do come true!

Bishop J. C. Parks

ONE

You could be the One

"And he dreamed yet another dream, and told it his brethren, and said, I have dreamed a dream more; and, behold, the sun and the moon and the eleven stars made obeisance to me (Genesis 37:9).

Everyone has had a dream at some point in his or her life. Whether you are young or old, rich or poor, everyone has had or will have at least one strong desire to achieve or accomplish a seemingly unreachable goal. The unreachable goal occupies our mind and thoughts. We feel that supernatural ability is required to achieve these goals. These seemingly unreachable goals or strong desires are our dreams.

I have had the distinct privilege of talking to Christians of difference races, backgrounds, nationalities, and countries. Most of them have or have had a dream. However, the difficulty for most of them is holding on to those strong desires, aspirations, or dreams. Over time their dreams seem to evaporate into just thoughts about the way things could have been.

The Apostle Paul's advice of pressing toward the mark of the high calling in Christ Jesus makes sense too many. However, the race seems too strenuous, and the finish line or mark seems too far away. They just throw up their hands; blame the devil, and say, "what's the use". Their dreams become wishful thinking and thoughts that never came to fruition.

Other Christians attempt to keep the faith, but are unsuccessful in persevering or holding on to their dreams. Their faith seems to fizzle with time. They never realize that holding on to their dreams is the greatest demonstration of faith. For dream achievement is what faith is really all about. Apostle Paul said,

Hebrews 11:1 clearly states that, "faith is the substance of things hoped for (dreams), the evidence of things not seen" (Hebrews 11:1).

Many Christians see the miracles of faith and prayer each day. They receive more blessings than they could have ever imagined. Nevertheless, they never achieve their dreams. Is this due to a lack of sincere faith? I have discovered that it is rather a lack of understanding.

One of my dreams was birth over 25 years ago in a little country church in Covington Tennessee. I was so excited that Sunday, because I was just accepted into the Engineering Program at Tennessee State University in Nashville Tennessee. By the grace of God, I received a four-year engineering scholarship from Tennessee State University. The scholarship arrived prior to the start of school. This was truly a blessing since my parents could not afford to pay for my college education. I had a strong desire to become a successful senior business executive; manage many hundreds of employees; and travel throughout the world. At that time, I was also struggling with my call into the ministry. Why was God calling me to preach the Gospel? The two directions seem to conflict with each other. I wasn't sure how God was going to help me achieve my career goals, and His plans for my life. But, I knew that I had favor with God. I constantly reminded myself that the Lord would make a way somehow.

So, I went to church that particular Sunday to give God praise for this unanticipated blessing. On my way to church, I also prayed and meditated about where God would take me next. What did God have in store for me?

Receiving that scholarship was truly a miracle. I felt that God was truly up to something. As the worship service began, I sat patiently listening and waiting for God to speak to my heart. I was anxiously waiting to hear the sermon by the late Pastor J. H. Tate.

Willing vessels were people that God could use to for His Glory.

God would always show willing vessels their destiny

Throughout my childhood, Pastor Tate was always an inspiration. Each Sunday he would seem to look for me after the church. Whenever I would talk to him, he would remind me to be a willing vessel for God. Pastor Tate was emphatic that willing vessels were people that God would use for His glory. God would always show willing vessels their destiny. When we are a willing vessel, we open our mind to the will of God. We trust God completely and firmly believe that He will keep His promises. Doubt and wavering faith are dismissed as an attack from the enemy. As a willing vessel, our mind is so focused on God that we only see our preordained destiny.

That particular Sunday, Pastor Tate preached from the 37th chapter and the 9th verse of the book of Genesis. This was the story of Jacob's youngest son Joseph. He had occasionally preached about Joseph over the years. He had preached about Joseph's struggles, his continual favor with God; and how God continually elevated him. However that Sunday, God used the story of Joseph to speak into my spirit a seed thought that would eventually change my life. In this particular scripture text, God had revealed to Joseph his destiny through dreams.

"And he dreamed yet another dream, and told it his brethren, and said, I have dreamed a dream more; and, behold, the sun and the moon and the eleven stars made obeisance to me" (Genesis 37:9).

Pastor Tate pointed out that God gives us instructions through our dream thoughts. Our dream thoughts were more than wishful thinking. Our dreams are thoughts inspired by our Divine Creator. Dreams were God's way of directing our steps toward our future. Job 33:15-17 states,

" In a dream, in a vision of the night, when deep sleep falleth upon men, in slumberings upon the bed; Then He openeth the ears of men, and sealeth

their instruction, that He may withdraw man from his purpose, and hide pride from man".

If we remain a willing vessel, God would give us proper instructions.

At the end of the worship service, Pastor Tate followed his normal custom of finding me before he left the church. He congratulated me on receiving the scholarship. He again reminded me to be a willing vessel, and never let go of my dreams. Pastor Tate reiterated a key point from his sermon. In the 41st verse of the 41st chapter of Genesis, he affirmed that God would always provide evidence that divine favor came by Him. God would make dreams come true.

As I drove home from the little wooden church that Sunday, I prayed fervently to become a willing vessel. I still had questions about my dreams. I knew that I had set goals for my life. Even though I had desires and persistent thoughts of my future plans, I had never thought of these as dreams that were inspired by God. Had God revealed to me my destiny through my dreams? Were my personal goals of becoming a business executive in a major company congruent with God's plan for my life? What about becoming God's messenger? I became somewhat perplexed about dreams. Pastor Tate's encouragement of becoming a willing vessel never departed from my heart. God would reveal to willing vessels their destiny.

In 1980, I graduated from college with an Engineering degree, and began my career with a major Fortune 500 company in my hometown area. While in college, I was called into the ministry. Shortly thereafter I became pastor of a small church in my hometown. After I graduated, the small church also began to grow rapidly. I had also quickly gained success and credibity within the company. I was content that I was in step with achieving both my personal and God's plan for my life. I had a successful career, and a growing ministry. I was living in my hometown with my family, relatives, and friends. I was beginning to travel, and see parts of the world that I had only read about.

One night while on my way home from work, I began to contemplate where God was going to take me next. Again, I pondered over my Pastor's points about Joseph's dreams. Had God already shown me my destiny through my dreams? Could my strong desire of becoming a successful business executive and pastor actually be instructions from God. I realized that only through faith would God reveal my ultimate future. Now, I realize that God divinely inspired these dreams. If I had not held onto these dreams, you would not be reading this book today.

Many Christians give up on their dreams. They give up because they think their dreams are their personal goals. They have not realized that God has predestinated us to become over-comers and abundantly blessed. We are also heirs of an inheritance. There are some things that are in our destiny to fulfill. God has created in us that "one thing" that will lead us to abundant living. God has placed in each of us a gift that could be used to achieve our dreams and ultimately His glory. We must learn to use that "one thing". Many Christians fail because they attempt to focus on their weaknesses. While this is required, we must learn how to build on our strengths. Joseph's gift was administrative ability. God placed Joseph in experiences to build on his strengths. So, you should ask God to reveal your strengths and build upon it. You will recognize your strengths. It will be a strong desire and where your passion lies.

Our choices, faith, and determination will determine the outcome of life's situation. Our ability to keep going, and patience will help us achieve the desires that God has birth in us. We will have to face many challenges before we achieve our dreams. Yet, we will understand that all of these things are necessary for us to develop a fuller understanding of God. These challenges will better prepare us to be a good steward of the blessings from our dreams.

So one day I thought, what is a dream? I picked up the Merriam Webster dictionary to find a clearer definition. The dictionary defined a dream as a vision of something possible, a goal, or purpose ardently desired; to consider a possibility. The word ardently means passionate, zealous, and devoted. Then, I realized that Paul's definition of faith was broader than I had thought, been taught, or had experienced in my life. Dream achievement is the evidence of my faith Things hoped for are our dreams, goals, desires, or possibilities. Hebrew 11:1 helped me make my view and understanding of dreams a lot clearer. In other words, Faith is the guarantee that our supernatural goals, or dreams will become a reality by devoting our ability; zealously letting God work through us; and passionately holding on until the dream happens. I felt a jolt of fire come up within me. I began to realize that my career and religious goals were divinely inspired dreams. These continual child-hood thoughts were merely reflections of my destiny preordained by God.

Faith is God's guarantee that our goal or purpose will be come a reality by devoting our ability, zealously letting God work through us; and passionately holding on to our dream.

Now that I better understood what faith was, I began to realize what God expected from me. I had to become passionate, zealous, and devoted to my dreams (things hoped for). This is true faith. God would use my decisions or thoughts to move me toward my inheritance. My dreams were part of my inheritance. Ephesians 1:11 states,

"In whom we have obtained an inheritance, being predestined according to the purpose of him who worketh all things after the counsel of His will:"

God has predetermined our future. Bad choices, decisions, and resulting circumstances only hinder us, but do not prevent us from achieving our divine purpose. All the great patriarchs and saints had a predetermined future.

At first glance, the patriarchs' destinies were a collection of mis-steps and bad decisions. However, the mighty hand of God was always working. Their challenge was to allow God to direct their every step. Solomon gives us good advice in the book of Proverbs. Solomon stated that everything is vanity. But, it is only God that we can trust and depend on. Proverbs 3:6 emphasizes the point,

"Trust in the Lord with all thine heart; and lean not to thine own understanding. In all thine ways acknowledge Him, and He shall direct your path".

God is committed to direct your path. However, God wants you to trust Him completely. God expects you to show appreciation and gratitude (acknowledgement) for His grace given to you.

The first step toward achieving your dreams is to first realize that you are pre-destined for greatness. This is one point that many Christians miss. They know that Jesus came that we might have life and have it more abundantly. Yet, they fail to see that the more abundantly represents achieving supernatural things. Your dreams should be bigger than a loving family, good job, car, house, clothes, and friends. Many Christians believe that these things represent the pinnacle of success. We must realized that this type of dream falls way short of what God wants us to achieve. Our personal goals will fall way short of the inheritance God has preordained for us.

As God put this revelation about dreams in my spirit, I began to study the steps that Joseph's approach to holding on to his dreams. God placed this particular story in the bible to show us his blueprint for achieving our destiny. Let's examine God's blueprint for Joseph.

At an early age, Joseph dreamed of his future. In verse 9 of the 37th chapter of Genesis, Joseph saw himself as God saw him. Joseph would become the head and not the tail. He would become above only and not beneath. Joseph said, "I have dreamed a dream more; and, behold, the sun and the moon and the eleven stars made obeisance to me." Joseph thoughts were more than just mere wishful thinking. Joseph realized that these were instructions from God. His family disregarded his comments, but God was affirming Joseph's destiny. Joseph saw himself as he would become.

You must begin seeing yourself as God sees you. See yourself being blessed exceeding abundantly above all that you can ask or think

How do you see yourself? You cannot just see yourself just being blessed. You must see yourself being blessed exceeding abundantly above all that you can ask or think. Isn't this what dreams are really about? They are not normal thoughts about achieving normal things. Dreams are thoughts about the achievement of supernatural things. Your dreams should exceed mere overachieving. If God inspires your dreams, they should be about achieving the impossible things.

Your dreams may seem unattainable at first glance. They may seem as wishful thinking and possibilities. However, you must begin to see yourself completely as God sees you. God sees beyond where you are. He knows your true potential. He allows tests to occur as part of your things development. Each test is designed to make you stronger, more confident, and closer to Him. If you don't resist and remain obedient to His will, you will achieve your success and destiny. The bible is filled with scriptures of how God sees you. In order for your dreams to be fulfilled, you must see yourself God's way. Its only when you see yourself God's way that God will begin to move you toward your inheritance.

Stop and meditate on this thought for a minute. You could be the one. You could be the one that God is waiting to unleash for His glory. There are so many powerful and anointed men and women of God. These notable Christians include Bishop TD Jakes, Billy Graham, Kenneth Copeland, Creflo Dollar, and Joyce Myers just to name a few. Have you ever listened closely to each of their testimonies? They all have dreams, but more than that. They each see themselves as God sees them. You should not discount your true potential. Your outcome will depend on how you feel about yourself. So, Why not you? God wants to do more than you can think or ask. It's according to the working of the power that is in you. You have to expand your faith to believe that you could be the one. Otherwise, God's instructions will not make sense to you.

You could be the one that God is waiting to unleash and use for His glory.

After Joseph's revelation, began to behave as if his dreams were already a reality, and not just a possibility. Joseph spoke with so much confidence that his brothers became envious of him. Joseph was so convinced that even Jacob his father Jacob became upset. Yet, Joseph's confidence made Jacob take notice of his son, and keep the matter in mind.

Most Christians have read or heard about positive thinking. But, God wants you to think with the power of the anointing. You must become familiar with the concept of Victory thinking. This kind of thinking is more powerful. Positive thinking attempts to motivate you to think positive about your possibilities. However, Victory thinking causes you to start your journey with the end in mind. You behave as if the outcome of your dream is a reality now. Victory thinking motivates you to talk about your future in the present tense. Victory thinking is truly walking by faith and not by sight. Victory thinking will prevent you from focusing on your present surroundings. You can only see the achievement of supernatural success.

Victory thinking is thinking and speaking with confidence of the outcome as though it is reality now

It was only through Victory thinking that the three Hebrew boys could stand fearless while facing a fiery furnace. It was Victory thinking that made Paul and Silas conduct a midnight revival while held captive in a Philippians jail. It was only through Victory thinking that John the Revelator remained faithful while being exiled on the Island of Patmos. Other great saints were born in poverty and oppression. It was Victory thinking that helped them overcome the odds.

Despite his obstacles and afflictions, Joseph never stopped thinking victory. Nowhere in the scriptures do you see Joseph being mired by his circumstances. As a matter of fact, each circumstance reinforced his resolve. Joseph received the favor of God because of his willingness to think victoriously. He knew that he could overcome by putting his total trust in the almighty God. So, how do you initiate

Victory thinking? It is really simple. It starts within your mind. It starts with faith. Remember my revelation on the definition of faith. Faith is the guarantee that our supernatural goal, or dream will become a reality by devoting our ability; zealously letting God work through us; and passionately holding on until the dream happens. When we begin to think victoriously, we devote our ability to the achievement of our dream, while zealously allow God to work through us. Then, God will reaffirm our thoughts through revelations by the Holy Spirit.

Through Victory thinking, you must think with confidence of a supernatural outcome. Your Victory thinking will be reaffirmed by revelations given to you by the Holy Spirit. I Corinthians. 2:9,10 states,

"Eye has not see, nor ear heard, neither have entered into the heart of man, the things which God hath prepared for them that love him. But God hath revealed them unto us by His Spirit; for the Spirit searcheth all things, yea, the deep things of God"

Once God shows you your destiny through the Holy Spirit, you must begin thinking, speaking, and preparing for your dreams. The power of Victory thinking will make your dream move toward you. The more passionately you think, speak, and act on them; and the more zealous you are about achieving it; will determine how fast they will happen.

Without a doubt, you could be the one. God has already declared that He is no respecter of person. God perfects His will through your thoughts and through your spoken word. The bible even tells us that God's angels await us to speak a word that will call them into action. You must think and speak of your dream in the present tense and not the future tense.. The bible says that we must, **"and calleth those things which be not as though they were" (Romans 4:17).** Joseph was so convinced that he began speaking his dream publicly. Joseph's thinking and speaking about his dreams reaffirmed his confidence in the God of promise. When you embrace Victory thinking, you are demonstrating true faith in God. Victory thinking motivates God to keep His covenants..

What did Joseph think and speak about? Joseph only thought and spoke about the outcome of his dreams. God didn't show him the steps to achieving his dreams. This is a wonderful thing. God will not reveal to you the steps for His master plan for your life. These steps are in the mind of God. Joseph would have never volunteered for his tribulation. However, it was his tribulation that created his opportunity. It was his opportunity that created his destination, and his destination took him to the achievement of his dreams.

When we are unaware of the steps to our dreams, we cannot interfere in God's plan. By nature, we always try to take control of our lives. We must restrain ourselves from this type of behavior. We have to learn to allow God to order our steps. Much of how we think is based on how we are taught. How have you been taught? We are taught to be proactive, and take charge of our lives. These principles are correct in achieving our personal plans. But, they often times hinder us in achieving our dream. Even though we may think that we have thought out the plan, God is still directing our every step.

Joseph didn't create a twelve-step plan for achieving his dreams. Joseph left those details to the Lord. Joseph had continual thoughts of supernatural success. Then, Joseph used every opportunity that God led him through to gain experience and spiritual maturity. Each experience or situation took him one step closer to his dreams. So, one of your greatest challenges will be to resist interfering in God's plan for your life. The Psalms 37:23 states,

"The steps of a good man or woman are ordered by the Lord, and he delighteth in his way".

God orders your steps. He determines the pace, hurdles, and milestones on your journey. Eventually, you learn to trust him completely. You learn that God knows what He is doing. God knows what is up ahead and He will lead you through it.

The more passionately you speak about your dream; and the more zealous you are toward achieving it; will determine how fast it will come to pass.

God knows where the curves are, and the trials that are necessary to increase your patience and your endurance. Your role is remain passionate, zealous and devoted to the dream. Remember, the revelation that God gave me on faith a few pages back The greatest demonstration of your faith is making your dream a reality by devoting ability, zealously letting God work through you; and passionately holding on to your dream. No matter what happens in your life, you must hold onto the dream. Despite all of the struggles, disappointments and trials, Joseph remained steadfast that God would work all things together for the good. You must be convinced that you will arrive at your appointed predestination. You must be determined that you could be the one. You could be the one that God is preparing to unleash into supernatural blessings. Those thoughts, desires, or inspirations have already been birth. Now, you must take the first step. You could be the one that will have the testimony about the achievement of supernatural success. Through your testimony and success, others will see that dreams do come true.

Before we continue with these revelations about Joseph's next steps, please review the Dream Notes and Dream Tool. Meditate on the thought that you could be the one. God is looking for willing vessels to give Him glory and honor. God is looking for someone to bless with supernatural blessings. Why not let this happen to you.

Dream Notes

➢ **Willing vessels are people that God can use to get glory. God will always show willing vessels their destiny.**

➢ **Faith is God's guarantee that our supernatural goals or purpose will be come a reality by devoting our ability, zealously letting God work through us; and passionately holding on to our dream.**

➢ **You must begin seeing yourself as God sees you. See yourself being blessed exceeding, abundantly above all that you can ask and think.**

➢ **You could be the one that God is waiting to unleash and use for His glory.**

➢ **Victory thinking is thinking, speaking, and behaving with confidence of the outcome as though it is reality now.**

Bishop J C Parks

Dream Tool

Use this dream tool to document your path to your dream. It will aid you in focusing upon what God really wants you to accomplish. Refer to this tool and use victory thinking on a monthly basis until you reach your dream. It will also help you be aligned with the will of God.

My Dream Is:
Describe a tangible view of your dream what God wants you to achieve

Succeed:
What will success look like?

Development:
What specifically should you do now?

God's Glory:
How will the achievement of your dream give God glory?

18

Two

Detours Can Lead to Destiny

"And Joseph was brought down to Egypt; and Potiphar an officer of Pharaoh, captain of the guard, and Egyptian, bought him of the hands of the Ishmaelite, which brought him down thither. And the Lord was with Joseph, and he was a prosperous man; and he was in the house of his master the Egyptian". Genesis 39:1,2.

It's amazing how God orchestrates our steps. Many times we stop to wonder. How did we get here? Each decision led to another situation. Each situation led to another person or opportunity. Most of the time we think that we are taking a detour away from our dreams.

After four years of success with my first position with a major Fortune 500 company. I was motivated to leave the company. There was really no good reason to leave. I was having a successful career. My managers and colleagues respected me. My first pastoral was also blessed with tremendous church growth. However, I felt pushed to leave all of these blessings. It was as if I was searching for something. My family, friends, and members were very concerned. Many asked me why I was attempting to leave my hometown, career, and pastoral. Some inquired or speculated about some personal problems. I would be leaving so much behind. God had truly blessed me. What else could a twenty-seven year old person want? Some would say that I had already achieved my dream. Others would say that my dream was already contained in that career and that church. Little did I know that the mighty hand of God was moving me in a new direction.

What at first could be seen as a detour was actually the second step toward my destiny. So, I left a successful career and pastoral. Within three weeks, I had joined another company and relocated to a city 350 miles away from my hometown in a small town in East Tennessee. Now, I had a new job and no church. It seemed as if I was starting my career all over again. I didn't know anyone, and had no relatives or friends in the area. The devil immediately attempted to convince me that I had made a mistake. Many of my friends fell by the wayside, as if I had committed a crime. I prayed fervently for God to keep me a willing vessel. Additionally, I remained faithful that God would direct my steps.

After joining my new company, I was promoted three times in four years. However, the four years were difficult times. I was the first African American to ever hold these managerial positions. I was challenged by jealousy and prejudices. Many thought that I was too young. Others were jealous because I had been promoted over them. There were even a couple attempts to assault me. I was assigned a major project. However, the project began to have serious problems. I was working 18 –20 hours a day. At times, I wondered why I had left my first company.

Also, I began to linger in my ministry. It took two years before I was a pastor again. God sent me to pastor a traditional church with many issues. The members were constantly in conflict with each other. These were difficult years. I was challenged by prejudice, frustrations of a small ministry, and possible failure in my new position, and my father was dying of cancer. However I remained faithful that God would keep me in His care.

The next year, my father died. His death was a very traumatic experience for me. My grandmother also died in the same year. I was working 18 hours a day, six days a week. My small church was only growing slightly. I was frequently sick, but I didn't stop trying. Some thought that I was failing. I was even criticized by my relatives and friend of my mistake to leave my hometown. I was working harder than I had ever worked. What started out as a good decision became a serious challenge.

However, one late summer evening I received a call from Barry Billerd to come to the Personnel office. He needed to talk to me about a concern. After arriving at his office, I was informed of another promotion to a senior manager's position. Once again, I would be the first African American to hold such a position. I was to relocate to Winston Salem, North Carolina within the next three weeks. Unfortunately, I had to resign as pastor of the small church. I resisted the urge to question God. I was determined to remain a willing vessel.

Relocating to Winston Salem, North Carolina several years ago allowed God to began a work in me that leads to many success stories. Moving to Winston

Salem was the third step toward my dreams. It was this move that led to me being promoted to a the highest-ranking African American in the company. God also blessed me to pastor a church that has changed the plight of a community. The church is beginning to be recognized for its ministries, deliverance, and becoming influential in effecting public policy. Many souls are being saved. Saints restored, and community enrichment is underway. Now, I see even clearer God's handiwork. My ten-year detour was part of my destiny.

It was during these last few years that a key revelation from Joseph's life was revealed to me. Detours can lead to destiny. What seemed like a detour to another company was actually positioning me. God was strategically moving me toward my destiny. He was deliberately directing me, so that one event would lead to another. My detour from my first thoughts of staying at home, having a successful career in my hometown, and being pastor of my hometown church, was all orchestrated by the mighty hand of God.

Most of us try to position ourselves for the best opportunities, best places, and with the best people. Normally, this approach is wasted effort. God creates the opportunity.   God had little David to carry lunch to his brothers, so that God could have David fight Goliath.   David's detour to the battlefield was the step toward his real destiny in the King's palace. Rejoice in every detour.   Each detour is an opportunity for God.

Examine the detour that Joseph took. Joseph was destined to become Governor of Egypt. His dream spoke of the sun, moon, and stars bowing down to him (Genesis 37:9). However, God did not catapult him into his destiny. He took a 13-year detour. Joseph's detours took him into a variety of difficult situations. Without knowing how the story would turn out, one would think that Joseph's dream was completely off track.

By nature, we try to avoid these types of trials, tribulation, and temporal afflictions. These things just don't feel good. However, detours are part of God's master plan. However, they serve a greater purpose. **James 1:2-4 says;**

"My Brethren, count it all joy when you fall into divers temptations; knowing this, that the trying of your faith worketh patience. But let patience have her perfect work, that you may be perfect and entire, wanting nothing."

The testing of your faith or detours helps you to develop perseverance. Perseverance makes you mature and complete lacking nothing. Your detours help your spiritual growth, so that you can gain the necessary experience and spiritual maturity.

Joseph had two major detours that led to his destiny. Joseph moved from being his father's pet to a pit. Then, Joseph's moved from being a slave to a servant. Joseph was Jacob's favorite. He was one of two sons birth by Jacob's wife Rachel, whom Jacob loved until her death. Joseph was given a coat of many colors as a testimonial of his father's love. Yet, it was these blessings that led to him being in a pit. However, please notice that the only way that Joseph could have arrived in Egypt in Pharaoh's house was to be placed in a pit by his brethren. Your pit is God's way of isolating you to get you on track. When you find yourself seemingly stuck in a seemingly hopeless situation, you should be rest assured that God is up to something. God is attempting to redirect you in some way. This is how God is positioning you for the next step in your journey to your dream.

Our detours help our spiritual growth, so that we can gain the necessary experience and maturity.

You must learn to accept where God has temporarily placed you. Your pit is only temporary. You must learn to be content until God gets ready to take you to your next steps. Paul tells us in Philippians 4:11,

"Not that I speak in respect of want: for I have learned, in whatsoever state I am, therewith to be content."

You must resist the urge to rationalize and figure out your own deliverance. God had to maneuver Joseph into the palace, so that Joseph would be in the right place. Joseph would never left Canaan on his own. Joseph was at home living comfortably with his entire family, and friends. But, Joseph's destiny was in the palace. It was Joseph's pit that led him to be isolated from the things and the people that could ultimately hinder him. So, God arranged for a journey into a pit. Interesting enough, it was the people closest to him that put him there. However, the mighty hand of God was working on his behalf.

Father's Pet to a Pit

This part of Joseph's life explains a lot of things. As Christians, we feel like our heavenly Father's pet. Our Heavenly Father always demonstrates to us that He loves us. He always treats us special. He blesses us despite our temperament or spiritual maturity. Most of our blessings are unexpected and undeserved. These blessings are God's way of giving us a coat of many colors. The coat of many colors shows our friend, family, co-workers, and community that we're special. We are anointed, appointed, and approved by God.. We rejoice in these things. We feel confident that God is with us. We hurriedly get to church just to praise Him and say thank you in a public assembly. We feel special to the point that we believe that little harm would ever come to us.

As our father's pet, we ask God for special privileges and blessings. God seems to answer our every prayer. He gives us favor that permits us to meet our goals effortlessly. We have friends, family, and favor. What else could a child ask of their father? Just when we go looking for an opportunity to follow our Father's will, our world changes dramatically. We find ourself in a pit. Many times we are placed there unaware. We blame the devil, people, or bad decisions. We feel isolated from our God. Our dream seems to stop in the pit. We cannot move forward. Every Christian must realize that God will always allow us to get into a pit. Our pit is not intended to harm us. It is intended to help us. I realize that my years of struggle were my pit. A pit will be on your journey toward achieving your dream. You should not even asked God why me? The devil will show up, while you are in your pit. He will make that you have done wrong or are lacking in your relationship with God. But, your pit is only temporary.

God uses our pits to isolate us, so that we can change direction.

While I was in my pit, people that was close to me assumed that I had made a bad decision. I had to stay in my pit until God was ready to deliver me. Every pit whether financial problems, issues with relationships, or health problems are a "pit" for His glory. God uses our pit to isolate us, so that we can change direction. God revealed to me other saints that He allowed to get into a pit, and become isolated, so that He could move them closer to their destiny.

- Moses' pit became the backside of a desert. Moses had to leave a plush palace to live forty years as a shepherd watching over someone else's sheep. However, it was at the backside of a mountain isolated, and seemingly going nowhere, that Moses met God. It was when Moses seemingly was isolated from his people that God could speak to Moses' heart. Then, God moved him to his ultimate assignment-Israel's deliverance.

- Jacob's pit was living in the desert far from home and his father's house. Jacob stole his brother's birthright and became a fugitive. He couldn't return home. However, it was in his isolation that he met God and received a blessing, and a divine name change to Israel.

The bible contains many resumes of people that God allowed to get in a pit, so that He could change their direction. So, whenever you find yourself in a pit, you should realize that God wants to isolate you, so that He can redirect your steps.

The Ishmaelite bought Joseph as a slave. When we are in a pit, we become a slave to whatever God is using to change us. We are captured and cannot be delivered, until the appointed time and place. Early in life, I thought these situations were of the devil. Then, the Holy Spirit revealed the difference to me. The revelation is also found in the story of Joseph. When God has captured you, you will not be harmed by the people that God is using. You may feel helpless, and lack control of the situation. However, you should remember that God has to capture you to carry you to your next steps. When the devil is involved, you will see destruction and calamity. Remember that the devil comes to kill, steal, and destroy. When you are captured by the devil, his will is that your life spirals on a downward plight to destruction. However, when God captures you, He is preparing you for a greater purpose. You may have to endure a temporal affliction, but favor is a still on your life. Verse 2 of the 39th chapter of Genesis reminds us that the Lord was with Joseph.

Slave to Servant

Notice that Joseph was taken to Egypt as a slave, but immediately became a servant in the place of his destiny. I had to learn this interesting fact about God. God always placed us in the place of our destiny to be a servant.

We must resist the urge to ask God why do we have to become a servant. Why does God locate us in certain places with certain types of people. In many respects, we may become a servant to people with less anointing, less gifts, and less favor with God. But, God has to teach us some things about servanthood. Upon arrival into Egypt, Potiphar, an officer of Pharoah, purchased Joseph as servant.

When I later read the latter part of verse two of the 39th chapter of Genesis, I received a powerful revelation from God, **" and he (Joseph) was in the house of his master the Egyptians"**. God connected Joseph to the right house. He gained knowledge, credibility, and became a man of integrity. This is what servanthood teaches us. You cannot simply arrive at your destiny without the proper knowledge and experience. God uses servant hood to teach you to become responsible, to refine your skills, and ability. Servant hood allows you to become credible with people, while your experience is growing. Without being a servant first, you will not properly be prepared to handle your position of leadership.

Look how God allowed Joseph to be prepared for his ultimate position. Genesis 39:4,6 says,

"And Joseph found grace in his sight, and he served him; and he made him overseer over his house, and all that he had out to his hand. Verse 6 says, "And he left all that he had in Joseph's hand; and he knew not ought he had, save the bread which he eat. And Joseph was a goodly person, and well favored".

Joseph learned how to oversee Potiphar's household and all of his possessions. Remember, God has to first prove that He can trust you with another man's riches before He will give you the true riches of your dream. This is part of servanthood training. Joseph was now well favored with all of Potiphar's household and acquaintenances. As you go through your training in servant hood, you must learn all you can.

God uses servanthood to teach us to become responsible, to refine our skills, and ability.

Remember, God uses all things working together for your good. Servant hood is also intended to humble you. You will experience your deepest emotions and levels of anxiety. Servant hood also helps others to see your growth. During this period, your skills and ability is being fine-tuned. Your experiences are being used to exact a perfect work in you. Without Servant hood training, you would not appreciate the blessings from God. More importantly, you would not be able to help others understand the benefits of trials and tribulations. A testimony without experience is like clouds with no rain. As you move through your phase of servant hood, you should rejoice

Joseph's experience in servant hood would be beneficial to him as he faced his greatest challenge. He would not have been equipped to administrate through a calamity without this experience. Without servant hood training, you would not be capable of sustaining your dream even in if even by happenchance that you achieved it. You should remember to disregard the circumstances, your surrounding, or the people you are associated with. Your motivation is to use servant hood training for a greater purpose.

Dream Notes

➤ **The more passionately you speak about your dream; and the more zealous you are toward achieving it; will determine how fast it will come to pass.**

➤ **Our detours help our spiritual growth, so that we can gain the necessary experience and maturity.**

➤ **God uses our pits to isolate us, so that He can change our direction.**

➤ **God uses servant hood to teach us to become responsible, to refine our skills, and ability.**

Dream Tool

Use this dream tool to document your path to your dream. It will aid you in focusing upon what God really wants you to accomplish. Refer to this tool and use victory thinking on a monthly basis until you reach your dream.   It will also help you be aligned with the will of God.

Lessons Learned
What detours have you taken thus far?

Successes and Failures
What have you learned from my detours?

Transition
How can God use your detours to
help you in your next steps toward your dream?

Three

Don't Let Obstacles Stop You

"And it came to pass after these things, that his master's wife cast her eyes upon Joseph; and she said lie with me....... And it came to pass, as she spake to Joseph day by day, that he hearkened not unto her, to lie with her, or to be with her. Genesis 39:7, 10

Joseph was goodly and well favored in Potiphar's house. Potiphar trusted Joseph with all of his possessions. Joseph could have become complacent, and thought that Potiphar's house was the achievement of his dreams. This is a trap for most Christians. They achieve the American dream, and become satisfied with their blessings. These Christians stop short of their true potential in the will of God. They have a job or career, people respect them, and they become content with their achievement. Some are amazed that they were able to make it thus far. When they compare themselves to other Christians, they clearly have surpassed the average Christian. What more could they ask for? They justify their contentment by rationalizing that God doesn't want us to be rich, or, the love of money is the root of all evil. So, they stop dreaming, become content, and never reach their true potential in the will of God. These people are also the ones who harbor regret later in their life. They finally realize that God wanted more for them. Usually, they see someone that had less natural ability exceed them. Unfortunately, they become unwilling to step out on faith, and reinvigorate their dream. They lack the motivation, confidence, and energy. Their dream simply evaporates.

We must understand that God is committed to us fulfilling our dream. If we are determined to persevere and stay within the will of God, we will receive the promise. For those people like Joseph who don't want to become complacent, they will continue to strive and excel having known God will elevate them to achieve even greater levels of anointing through Him. God is able to do exceeding abundantly above all that you can ask or think. But, this type of anointing is based on the power that is within you. As a Christian, you must maintain your integrity. You must completely understand that accomplishing your dreams glorifies God. The bible says in Matthews 16:19,

If we are determined to persevere and stay within the will of God, we will receive the promise.

"So, let your light so shine that men may see your good works and glorify God in heaven".

When you excel in abundant good works or the accomplishment of your dreams, God gets the glory out of your life. Then, God gives you back blessings, press down, shaken together, and running over. Then, others begin to see what God has done for you. Your blessings are intended to help increase someone's faith in God.

If you do not stop and dwell at the crossroad of complacency, the next steps on the journey to your dreams is the trying of your faith.. God will evaluate our faith in Him. So, God allows obstacles to test you. So, what does God test? God tests our patience, and self control. **Hebrews 10:36 says,**

"For ye have need of patience, that, after ye have done the will of God, ye might receive the promise".

God uses obstacles to test and build our patience. The obstacles are the trying of our faith. God wants to see whether we will stay within His will. Many times we fail the test. So, God allows us to see the same obstacles again and again until we overcome them.

"For ye have need of patience, that, after ye have done the will of God, ye might receive the promise".

Many Christians give up at this point and begin to accept the status quo. Their testimonies are outdated, and they speak of things that happen many years ago. Many become disillusioned with God, while they watch others achieving their dream. They become very bitter. They believe that God has let them down. However, those who see themselves in their dream and realize that God is testing them will persevere. They realize that God is always testing their perseverance. Even though we are anointed, appointed, and approved, we must pass the temptations and trials set before us

Verse 7 of the 39th chapter of Genesis says, **"and it came to pass after these things, that.."** And it came to pass suggest some kind of prearranged situation that God was allowing to happen. God created a hedge around Joseph while he was gaining favor and control of Potiphar's house. The bible now indicates something came to pass. After these things, the blessings and favor had materialized in Joseph's life. Then, it came to pass. God always evaluate what choices we will make. God wants to know will we maintain our integrity, and remain tenacious toward achieving our dream. So, the first test is always a test of patience. Would Joseph remain devoted to God and Potiphar? So, it came to pass.

Obstacles will take one of three forms: lust of the flesh, pride, or fear.

God knew that obstacles could distract or sidetrack Joseph. If Joseph did not possess patience, he would fail. In my life experiences, I have learned that every major obstacle was an opportunity for me to become distracted, become sidetracked, or simply give up. God allows the devil to construct these obstacles for a greater purpose. The devil's ultimate desire is for us to stop us.

These obstacles will take one of three forms: lust, of the flesh, pride, or fear. The devil will use one or all of these obstacles to exploit our weaknesses. Throughout the bible these three obstacles show up. Even in the temptation of Jesus in the wilderness. The fourth chapter of Matthews details the obstacles that Satan used against Jesus. It is very important on your journey to your destiny that you familiarize yourself with Satan's obstacles. Satan said in Matthews 4 chapter,

"If thou be the Son of God, command that these stones be made bread" (Lust of the Flesh).

"If thou be the Son of God, cast thyself down; for it written, He shall give his angels charge concerning thee; and in their hands they shall bear thee up, lest at any time thou dash thy foot against a stone" (Fear).

"And he saith unto him, All these things will I give thee, if thou wilt fall down and worship me." (Pride)

There are many more examples throughout the bible revealing these three obstacles as Satan's major weapons. The devil attempts to show God that his investment in and love for us is futile.

Take a minute to think about your obstacles. You should be able to categorize all of your trials, tribulations, or tests in one of these three categories. Remember, the devil has no new tricks. The Apostle

Paul advises us to not be ignorant of the devil's devices.

"Lest Satan should get an advantage of us; for we are not ignorant of his devices" (2 Cor. 2:11).

Therefore, we must always be watchful and prayerful of these obstacles.

Examine again verse seven of the thirty-ninth chapter of Genesis in Joseph's story; and it came to pass. When ever you see these words in Holy Scripture, it is an indication of some temporary event. The event came to pass. It did not come to stay. This is God way of letting you know that you can prevail through your obstacles. No temptation or test comes to stay. The obstacle is God way of allowing you to grow in maturity. You have to maintain complete and unwavering faith in God. Your goal ought to be to increase your patience. Patience will help you endure each and every obstacles. Let's examine these three obstacles in Joseph's journey to his dream.

Pride

Joseph could have yielded to pride. Look at his accomplishment in just a few years.

- He was promoted from slave to servant in Potiphar's house. The Lord was with Joseph and blessed him greatly in all of his endeavors.

- Joseph became Potiphar's favorite. Potiphar soon put Joseph in charge of his entire household and entrusted him with all of his business.

- The Lord blessed Potiphar for Joseph's sake. So, Potiphar gave Joseph complete administrative authority over everything that he owned.

Joseph could have easily yielded to pride. As a youth, he had a deep-seated pride. Joseph was babied, pampered, and spoiled. All of this had apparently gone to Joseph's head. His pride led to his brothers planning to murder him. Many times pride leads us to believe that our gift or ability has created an opportunity. We thank God for the blessings, but we praise ourselves for the accomplishment. It is so easy to believe that our hard work made us successful.

Pride is the root and essence of sin. The fall of Adam and Eve was centered on pride. Adam and Eve desired to be "as the gods". Pride is seeking for oneself the honor and glory that properly belongs to God. Pride is being conceited concerning one's talents, ability, wealth, or position in life. Pride always leads to disdainful behavior and disobedience. It was pride that caused the devil and one third of the heaven's host of angels to be kicked out of heaven.

The devil uses pride because he knows how God feels about pride. Proverbs 8:13 says,

"The fear of the Lord is to hate evil; pride, and arrogancy, and the evil way, and the froward mouth, do I hate".

God hates pride. We must beware of the obstacle of pride. Pride puts us at odds with God. It will cause us to lose the favor of God. Pride is the ringleader of many other sins. For pride lies up within our heart. So, God used Joseph's struggles to help him rid himself of pride. It was Joseph's struggles that caused him to replace his pride with a humble spirit. Regardless of your success, always acknowledge that God is the source and sustainer of all good and perfect gifts.

Lust of the Flesh

The second obstacle is the lust of the flesh. Satan will always appeal to our flesh. He will tempt us to yield through temptations or pressures. Lust of the flesh is any intense desire that becomes excessive or misdirected.   It may be concentrated on money, personal power, or sensual pleasures, such as sexual experiences and drunkenness. Again, Satan used this same obstacle on Adam and Eve. Genesis 3:6 says,

"And the woman saw that the tree was good for food, and that it was pleasant to the eyes, and a tree to be desired to make one wise, she took of the fruit thereof , and did eat, and gave also unto her husband with her; and he did eat".

The tree was pleasant to the eyes and created the temptation. The temptation turned into lust. So, lust of the flesh is a key weapon of Satan

In Joseph's case, he was tempted by Potiphar's wife to have sex. Potiphar's wife kept tempting and putting pressure on him day after day. Joseph refused to sleep with her, and he kept out of her way, as much as possible. Sometimes merely trying to say no to the temptation is not enough. We must be watchful and avoid the temptation completely, especially when the temptation is strong and persistent. Joseph resisted the temptation by acknowledging that it would be a sin against God. Joseph could not disobey God. He would destroy his relationship with God. Joseph proved to God that he could be trusted more and more in higher positions of leadership.

Under pressure, excuses are easily rationalized away. Remember, the devil's intention is to create disobedience to God. Disobedience to God separates us from the favor of God. This is how we become hindered or sidetracked away from our dreams. Yielding to the lusts will create strongholds, and ultimately war with the soul.

"Dearly beloved, I beseech you as strangers and pilgrims, abstain from fleshly lusts, which war against the soul;" (I Peter 2:11).

Joseph was made stronger through this persistent temptation. God allowed Joseph to be tempted, so that he could learn self-denial, and self-control. Lust of the flesh attempts to rob us of control of our body, thoughts , and sanctification.

Fear

The third obstacle that hinders us from reaching our dream is fear. Fear paralyzes us, and demonstrates a lack of faith. Fear is the opposite of faith. God promotes faith, and the devil promotes fear. Many Christians stop on their journey to their dream due to fear. They become fearful of the outcome, or possible tragedy. They are unwilling to confront those things that are attempting to hinder them. Public opinion or the desire to have no pain makes them walk cautiously in every endeavor.

Joseph's real test occurred after he was successful. He would have to make decisions that either would lead him to his dreams, or become sidetracked. Becoming successful does not eliminate your fears. Success creates the opportunity for fear to exploit your faith. Joseph could have become fearful of Potiphar'' wife and yielded to her seduction. Joseph was in a serious predicament. What was he to do? If he submitted and yielded to Potiphar's wife, he probably could have gain a great advantage that could result from her favor. But, if he refused her, he could know her wrath. He could ultimately lose all of the blessings that had been awarded to him. I would imagine that Joseph had to contemplate his course. Saying no to Potiphar's wife could lead to imprisonment or death.

One day, all of the men servants were not available in the house. When Joseph entered in the house to perform his daily business, Potiphar's wife grabbed him and propositioned him. To deny her probably would have meant arousing her wrath and vengeance.

However, Joseph ran out of the house. Joseph fled so quickly that she yanked his cloak off.

Sometimes, Christians are seduced by the devil through fear. These Christians begin to feel that they will end up losing something valuable. So, the devil takes advantage of their fear. The devil attempted to use fear on Job, a perfect and upright man. In the book of Job, Job said that the thing that he feared had come upon him.

"For the thing which I greatly feared is come upon me, and that which I was afraid of is come unto me" (Job 3;25)

Fear is not of God. The bible says that God has not given us the spirit of fear. Fear of failure or destruction should be replaced with confidence in God.

Psalms 23:4 say, "Yea though I walk through the valley of the shadow of death, I will fear no evil".

The obstacle of fear is one of the greatest weapons of Satan. The devil knows that without faith, it is impossible to please God. Unfortunately, fear normally comes when we speak it into existence. You cannot talk and walk in fear. Whatever you fear will come upon you. When you have faith, you believe God. When you have fear, you believe in the devil.

Fear does not come from God. Because scripture says, God has given us the spirit of love, power, and a sound mind. We can only overcome the obstacle of fear by completely trusting in God. Not yielding to our fears, may create new trial for us.

However, the God of promise will always make a way to escape it.

Joseph was able to confront all of his obstacles. This is a crucial part of holding on to your dreams. Your willingness to face your obstacles and deal with them, will determine your ultimate outcome. If you attempt to move around your obstacles, it will result in delay. Eventually, you will be faced with the same obstacles that you attempted to avoid. This is part of God's process of maturing us. So, you should plan to face your obstacles. If you wrestle with them, you will overcome them by the power of God.

Dream Notes

- ➢ **Obstacles will take one of three forms: lust of the flesh, pride, or fear.**

- ➢ **Learn to face your fears. You're not alone.**

- ➢ **God wants to know will we maintain our integrity, and remain tenacious.**

- ➢ **Success creates the opportunity for fear to exploit your faith.**

Dream Tool

Use this dream tool to document your path to your dream. It will aid you in focusing upon what God really wants you to accomplish. Refer to this tool and use victory thinking on a monthly basis until you reach your dream. It will also help you be aligned with the will of God.

Lessons Learned
Which of the three Obstacle(s) are intending to hinder you?

Successes and Failures
How will God allow you to overcome your obstacles?

Transition
How is God leading you to overcome your obstacles?

Four

God is Always Up to Something

"And Joseph's master took him, and put him into the prison, a place where the king's prisoners were bound; and he was there in the prison. But the Lord was with Joseph, and shewed him mercy, and gave him favor in the sight if the keeper of the prison. And the keeper of the prison committed to Joseph' Genesis 39:7, 20-22.

Clearly, God was using Potiphar's wife for a purpose. Interesting enough Joseph was already in Potiphar's house, but was not noticed by his wife. However, it was, after these things, that she cast her eyes upon Joseph. The temptation came after Joseph was established as a goodly person and well favored. Joseph resisted the temptation, and did not yield to fear, pride, or the lust of the flesh.

Now, Joseph had to suffer the trial of lies and false accusations. Potiphar's wife was a woman in rage. She turned against Joseph and rejected him. She set out to humiliate him and hurt him as much as she could. She attempted to create prejudice against him as a Hebrew. She also attempted to destroy his reputation and character, by stating that he had raped her. Joseph now suffered the loss of everything that he had gained; his possessions and position. Potiphar's wrath fell upon Joseph. Joseph was imprisoned and placed in fetters and irons. Joseph was cast into political prison. Potiphar placed Joseph in the prison where he was in charge and the overseer. (Genesis 40:3). Potiphar had no intentions of ever releasing him.

Joseph had to have questioned God about the injustice of his imprisonment. He had obeyed God and done the right thing. He had not yielded to pride, fear, or lust of the flesh. He had demonstrated to Potiphar that he was a man of integrity. Why would Potiphar not believe him? Why didn't God do something to keep him out of prison. Joseph had already borne the grief and agony of being sold as a slave and brought to Egypt. But now, his situation was far worse. Joseph was now a prisoner. Even though Joseph demonstrated consistent faith, hard work, obedience, and flawless integrity.

Joseph learned a valuable lesson about endurance and hardship. In future years, he would be chief administrator over all of Egypt. He was to have complete control over the food supply. To be a just and compassionate administrator, he would have to know what it felt like to lose everything. This was a lesson that Joseph had to learn and learn well. Compassion, endurance, and hardness would all be necessary to lead Egypt through its economical collapse. Egypt would be faced with a seven year famine.

We will all experience this type of suffering at one time or another. Sometimes, it seems like God is leading us into a trap. We go from a successful situation to calamity. It happens so fast that we wonder how did this happen. The calamity comes in strange ways that makes no sense. It's the doctor's prognosis of a serious disease when we're in peak condition. It's the closing of a company, after we have established ourselves with a successful career track. It is the loss of a loved one or divorce. These situations of suffering will occur on your way to achieving your dreams.

One of the greatest revelation that I have had while persevering toward my dream is that God is always up to something. God has an agenda for our lives. God will make sure that we are properly prepared to handle every situation in our future. He proves us each step of the way. He tests to see whether we can be faithful over the small things, before He can elevates us to greater things.

Every level that we climb becomes more challenging. These tests grow from small trials to sufferings. I have had to learn that God is not tempting us, but testing us. Just like a High School teachers gives tests to their students, God gives us tests. The High School teachers use the tests to calibrate whether we have learned all of the vital elements of the subject. God works in a similar way. However, these tests are not for His benefit. God tests are to help us determine our spiritual maturity. When we awaken to the reality that

God will make sure that we are properly prepared to handle every situation in our future.

we fall short, we attempt to get closer to God. We seek Him out, and gain even greater trust in Him.

God was up to something with Joseph. God was preparing Joseph by teaching him to have a positive attitude while dealing with severe circumstances. As Christians, we must understand that some suffering is required on our journey to achieving our dream. God use suffering to make settle us, and to strengthen us. I Peter 5:10 states,

"But the God of grace, who hath called us into His eternal glory by Christ Jesus, after that ye have suffered a while, make you perfect, stablish, strengthen, settle you."

This scripture is such a wonderful revelation. Suffering is intended for our good. Suffering matures, and settles, and strengthens us.

God strengthen Joseph and helped him to become settled. Joseph learned to maintain a positive attitude, which lead to a deeper trust and commitment to God. prison, Joseph learned the qualities of leadership in hard and difficult times. You cannot be fair-weather Christians. You should try to remain steadfast and unmovable through your difficult times. Your difficult times might last for few weeks or a few years. However, you have to learn that the longer the suffering, the greater the reward.

> *"But the God of grace, who hath called us into His eternal glory by Christ Jesus, after that ye have suffered a while, make you perfect, stablish, strengthen, settle you."*

The warden of the prison began to notice Joseph.

The warden saw that Joseph was a capable and a hard worker. The warden also noticed that Joseph's God blessed everything Joseph did. Therefore, the warden made Joseph overseer over all of the other prisoners.

Having strong determination demonstrates that God will bless us no matter where we are and irregardless of our trials and circumstances

Please notice that Joseph was in the lowest position that a man can find himself in jail.

Joseph shows us the benefit of trusting in God and holding on to your dream, even in severe circumstances. His strong determination demonstrates that God will bless us no matter where we are and irregardless of our trials and circumstances. God blessed Joseph and made everything he did a success.

So, you must believe God and His word. God will use the trials of your life and your blessings to make you better. More importantly, God wants you to become a good steward of your dreams. Therefore, you should count it all joy when your suffering comes. It will make you a better person, better family member, better citizen, better co-worker, and a better Christian. Upon achieving your dream, you will be a wonderful steward of what God has provided for you. Your suffering may seem difficult. But, you should not lose focus. While going through your suffering, you must not stop and become discouraged. You must get up and go to work. You must work even harder and more diligently than those around you. Colossians 3:23-24 states,

"Whatsoever ye do, do it heartily, as to the Lord, and not unto men; knowing that of the Lord ye shall receive the reward of the inheritance; for ye serve the Lord Christ"

In your suffering, you have to be a person of high character with a great positive attitude. You must know and believe that God is using your suffering to prepare you for something greater—your dream.

God was also up to something else. God had to make sure that Joseph remained successful in all kinds of situations. God was also preparing Joseph to be second in rule in Egypt. Then and only then would the Egyptians allowed Jacob and his family to settle in Goshen. God could thereby fulfill his promise to Abraham, Isaac, and Jacob. God promised Abraham that he would be a great nation. Joseph's progression toward his dream was also an instrument that God was using to fulfill a promise.

Each of our lives touches someone else's. Everything that we do can and will affect someone else's destiny. Our unwillingness to pursue our dreams hinders God from achieving all of His purposes. When we are tempted to stop or not even start making, we are hindering God from working a greater plan.

"For our light affliction, which is but for a moment, worketh for us a far more exceeding and eternal weight of glory; while we look not at the things which are seen, but at the things which are not

seen; for the things which are seen are temporal; but the things which are not seen are eternal" (**2 Corinthians 4:17-18).**

We must understand that the fulfillment of our dreams is only the means to an end. God is a God of promise. If we be in Christ, we are Abraham's seed. Therefore, the fulfillment of our dreams allows God to keep His promise to Abraham. God sealed this promise to Abraham in a blood covenant. This means that God cannot change His mind, and not fulfill His promise. Both heaven and earth can pass away, but God's word cannot change. This is the confidence that we should have about our dreams. Since God promised Abraham that his seed would be blessed, we have a guarantee that God will allow us to achieve our dreams.

When you are moving toward the fulfillment of your dreams, you must remind yourself that God is up to something. God is attempting to perform a greater work through you. God is wanting to use those things that He has planted and invested in you for the fulfillment of His promise. You have been selected by God as a vessel to be used for the Master's will and glory. What a wonderful blessing!. You should come to the revelation that God is using you to accomplish His divine will. The achievement of your dreams allows His will to come to pass. To God be the glory!

Dream Notes

➤ **God will make sure that we are properly prepared to handle every situation in our future.**

➤ **Having strong and solid determination demonstrates that God will bless us no matter where we are and irregardless of our trials and circumstances.**

➤ **Each of our lives touches someone else's. Everything that we do can and will affect someone else's destiny.**

➤ **When we are tempted to stop or not even start making our dreams become a reality, we must realize that God is working a greater plan.**

Bishop J C Parks

Dream Tool

Use this dream tool to document your path to your dream. It will aid you in focusing upon what God really wants you to accomplish. Refer to this tool and use victory thinking on a monthly basis until you reach your dream.   It will also help you be aligned with the will of God.

Lessons Learned
What is God up to in your life?

Successes and Failures
How has your suffering prepared you for something greater?

Transition
How will you use your suffering to allow God to work his greater purpose?

Five

Learn How to Wait for Your Success

"Yet did not the chief butler remember Joseph, but forgat him." Genesis 40:23.

Joseph was prosperous while in prison. The Lord showed him mercy, and gave him favor with the warden of the prison. The Warden placed Joseph as overseer of all activities in the prison. Joseph was also responsible for all of the prisoners. Whatever was done in the prison was done under Joseph's supervision. Neither did the Warden check up on Joseph. Basically, Joseph ran the prison. Only the loving hands of God could make this happen. However, God had to teach Joseph a lesson on waiting. God used Joseph's prison experience to teach him to forgive and to wait patiently for God's time.

It is very difficult to wait. By nature, we want instant gratification, a quick response, and a speedy recovery. We are even taught to be proactive and to make things happen quickly. Our success in our careers is based on our ability to get results. Usually, the expectation is to obtain these results in short order. We are also taught to be competitive. We must hurry up, so that we can beat our competition for the next promotion, or job assignment. However, God does not seem to be impressed with our rush to get these things done.

God's nature is to do everything decently and in order. He takes no shortcuts. Even when we are going through our suffering, it seems as if God is taking His time. We occasionally ask, why does it take God so long? If God could create the world in six days, why does it take months and even years for God to move in our lives? What is holding up the fulfillment of our dream?

Despite his success, Joseph remained in prison. He was no doubt suffering in chains for a long time. Potiphar was in charge of the prison. It was Potiphar's wife that Joseph supposedly had attacked. The Warden noticed Joseph's hard work over the period of time, before he would have made him overseer of the other prisoners. Now, just think of the suffering, pain, and agony of having his feet and ankles shackled with fetters and chains. Even though he was later taken out of the chains, he was still in prison. Why was Joseph still in prison? Shouldn't his accomplishments and effort have given him a prison release? Why would God allow such a thing to continue? These are questions that we have all asked as we continue to go through our struggles.

The importance of the virtue of learning how to wait cannot be overemphasized. Waiting allows God to accomplish an even greater work in us. God has a plan. His plan is to spend whatever time necessary to "prune us". The time required for God "to prune" is dependent upon us. When we are willing to seek God's guidance, he keeps our steps. Occasionally, we become doubters, hasty, and seek ways for solving our own problems. Then, we become stalled and make no progress. Learning to wait makes us perfect. God make us wait to accomplish molding our nature into the into his own image. We cannot truly fulfill our dream, until we take on the nature of God.

Waiting teaches us humility, courage, and more patience.

Pharaoh imprisoned his chief butler and chief baker in the Pharaoh's prison. Both men were chief officials in their own areas, and worked within Pharaoh's palace. Joseph was assigned the duty of serving and caring for their needs. He served them for a long time. The bible indicates that Joseph served them for a season. (verse 4), while he was waiting.

Why does God make us wait?. Waiting teaches us humility, courage, and forgiveness.

Humility

God used Joseph's prison experience to teach him the importance of being humble and asking for help. Joseph was made stronger through humility. In verse 14, Joseph asked the cupbearer to remember him, to show kindness, and for the cupbearer to ask Pharaoh for his release. Earlier in life, Joseph had pride, arrogance, deceit, and haughtiness. Joseph's father favored Joseph's over his brother because of his unusual management ability. Jacob had made Joseph overseer his other brothers, despite his young age. So,

God had to humble Joseph's heart and season his character. This is what was happening as God made Joseph to wait for his release from prison. God was creating within Joseph a contrite spirit.

A person of humility realizes his imperfections and acknowledges that all of his goodness, accomplishments, and good works to God's grace

Humility is an absolute necessity in life. The humble person does not attribute to himself any goodness or virtue that he does not possess. He does not overate himself or take immoderate delight himself. A person of humility realizes his imperfections, and acknowledges that all of his goodness , accomplishments, and good works comes from God's grace. Proverbs 16:19 states,

"Better it is to be of an humble spirit with the lowly, than to divide his spoils with the proud."

You will never achieve your dreams unless you have a true spirit of humility. When God has you waiting, he is teaching you to learn humility. As a Christian, you have just as many shortcomings as others. You should never walk around with a spirit of pride or arrogance. Not a single one of us is better than the other; no matter what our gift or level of anointing. When you learn how to wait, you are letting your prisons of suffering humble you. You should not be concerned about defeat or humiliation. While you are enduring, God is continually watching over you.

God commands us to be humble. Romans 12:3 says,

" For I say, through the grace of God of given unto me, to every man that is among you, not to think of himself more highly than he ought to think; but to think soberly, according as God hath dealt to every man his measure of faith".

Even Christians exaggerate about their blessings. They want others to think that they have the favor of God. They purchase new cars, house, and other tangible assets to demonstrate their relationship with God. Many times, they are incapable of paying for these things. They become indebted and suffer needlessly. Proverbs says that the blessings of the Lord maketh rich, and has no sorrow. This is the true test of whether God has given us favor. When we do not have a humble spirit, God sees this behavior as pride. Therefore, you must accept your current status. Because your current status is only temporary. God is capable of elevating you in due season. However, God wants you to acquire humility.

Jesus demonstrated the highest level of humility. Jesus was willing to leave His home in glory, and suffer the shame of the cross for us. Jesus allowed the Lord to use him completely. Even though He was God, He was tempted and suffered as we do. Now, He is sitting on the right hand of the God. This is the type of humility that God requires of us. God uses our suffering to create this type of humility. God will continue to incubate us until we become humble. I have witnessed many people experience extreme suffering. They loss completely everything, including their health. They cried out and prayed to God, but maintained their pride. Eventually, God broke their high minded spirit. After being humbled, God used them as a living testimony and example of a model Christian.

Humility proves to God our intentions. God rewards the humble in spirit. With humility comes riches, honor, and life. **"By humility and fear of the Lord are riches, honour, and life." (Proverbs 22:4).**

Humility allows us to press forward energetically without thought of self or admiration from the world

Humility brings with it true religion, which is expressed by the fear of the Lord. Pride hinders true religion. The feeling of dependence, a lowly opinion of self, and the surrender of the will is the fear of the Lord. The fear of the Lord is the source of every blessing. Humility is difficult to acquire. It is so essentially different than weakness. Humility allows us to press forward energetically without thought of self or admiration from the world. We are rewarded with riches, honor, and life. When justice is done, the best man will receive the best reward. The humble that do not seek honor shall have it. The first shall be last, and the last shall be first.

Courage

Joseph was made stronger through courage. God used his prison experience to teach him about truth. When the chief baker inquired about the interpretation of his dream, Joseph gave him a truthful interpretation. Joseph told the chief baker that he would die within three days. This act by Joseph took a lot of courage. Most likely, the chief baker had become Joseph's friend. However, Joseph had gain courage by learning how to wait. We often face situations that require us to share bad news. At such times, we must remain courageous and truthful. We must not deceive people and have them living on false hope. We must help them to have hope in God. Learning to wait is an essential to gaining courage. God uses our waiting to show us that our difficult circumstance will not overcome us. Overcoming our difficult situation builds courage. Psalms 118:6 says,

" The Lord is on my side; I will not fear; what can man do unto me?

We discover through waiting that God was with us all the time.

Patience

Joseph was made stronger through his disappointments. Joseph's prison experience taught him to forgive and wait patiently for God's time. Joseph's interpretation of the chief baker and chief cupbearer came to pass. The chief baker was hanged, and the chief cupbearer was restored to his former position. However, the chief cupbearer forgot. The scripture did not say why the chief cupbearer forgot about Joseph. Joseph had to remain in prison for two more long years. These two years must have been the most difficult years of all. Joseph must have had high expectations about being released from prison. Every time the prison doors were opened, he had to expect that his deliverance had come. However, Joseph was forgotten in prison. He had to finally accept that the cupbearer was not going to help him. He would not get a chance to appeal his case before Pharaoh.

Joseph could have easily become depressed and despondent. The chief cupbearer was someone in high places who had the power to help him, but he forgot about Joseph immediately after being released from prison. This type of treatment had occurred before in Joseph's life. The people closest to him had failed him: his brothers, Potiphar, and now the chief cupbearer. They all had failed and disappointed him. But God would use these disappointments to teach him the art of learning to have patience. Notice that the bible does not indicate that Joseph made any complaints. He never spoke to Potiphar about his wife's behavior, or the charge of rape. Joseph remained silent. He was learning to forgive and wait patiently on God. God was supplying Joseph strength in his time of trouble. The bible says,

"Wait upon the Lord; be of good courage, and he shall strengthen thine heart; wait, I say, on the Lord" (Psalms 27:14).

God will strengthen your heart to be able to handle any difficult situation. You should expect God to deliver you. However, God expects you to wait until His appointed time.

Think how often those closest to you have hurt and cause you pain. How often they may forget you and fail you. These people also sometimes mistreat you, and caused suffering to occur in your life. Many times, the worst offenders are those in the body of Christ. Some Christians have made promises that they didn't or can't keep. They consistently fall short of your expectations. In many cases, these disappointments come from the people that you have helped or loved the most. They apologize to you, and continue to let you down. Paul letters to the New Testament church applies to many of our churches today. You must learn to forgive when people forget you and mistreat you. You must learn to wait on God, and not wait on people. These people include your loved ones, friends, and close acquaintances. People can help sometimes, but not always. Even if they help, they cannot always meet your need. The only perfect help that is available for all circumstance is help of God. You must learn to wait patiently upon Him.

You cannot rush your dreams. Learning to wait teaches you to have peace and contentment. Waiting is holding on to the dreams. You must be determined to allow God's plan to work out. God will not speed up your dreams by your anxiousness. God will not indicate when your dreams will be fulfilled. He just guarantees that it will happen. Paul in Galatians advises us to be not weary in well doing, for we shall reap, if we don't give up. Not giving up is a key ingredient to holding on to your dreams. Dreams do come true. But there is normally a time element. God has so many things that He must orchestrate to ensure that you are at the right place at the right time. Learning how to wait ensures that you don't move prematurely in trying to accomplish your dreams. Waiting demonstrates your confidence in God. God will always keep His promise in His own time.

Dream Notes

- **Waiting teaches us humility, courage, and more patience.**

- **A person of humility realizes his imperfections and acknowledges that all of his goodness, accomplishments, and good works to God's grace.**

- **Humility allows us to press forward energetically without thought of self or admiration from the world**

- **Overcoming our difficult situation builds courage.**

- **God will not indicate when your dream will be fulfilled. He just guarantees that it will happen.**

Dream Tool

Use this dream tool to document your path to your dream. It will aid you in focusing upon what God really wants you to accomplish. Refer to this tool and use victory thinking on a monthly basis until you reach your dream. It will also help you be aligned with the will of God.

Lessons Learned
What have you learned by waiting?

Successes and Failures
What virtue is God attempting to strengthen in your waiting?

Transition
How is your waiting a benefit to God's greater plan?

Six

Dreams Do Come True

"And Pharaoh said unto Joseph, see I have set thee over all the land of Egypt. And Pharaoh took off his ring from his hand, and out it upon Joseph's hand, and arrayed him in vestures of fine linen, and put a gold chain about his neck; and he made him to ride in the second chariot which he had; and they cried before him, Bow the knee; and he made him ruler over all the land of Egypt." Genesis 41:41-44.

Joseph was strengthened to endure prison for two additional years. he had learned some valuable lessons in Egypt. He had a better perspective on life, and closer relationship with God. He discovered that detours do lead to destiny. God had ordered his steps. Joseph also learned that obstacles will not stop you, because God is always up to something. His most valuable lesson was learning to wait. He was held captive in prison while the chief cupbearer was set free. Joseph had proven to God that he was now ready. He had been "pruned" , and was now ready for his dream his success.

Earlier in this little book, I mentioned that God prunes us. God works to purgeth and strengthen us. We cannot escape God's effort to prune us. He intends to make us more productive. God will not give us our dreams, so that we could become unproductive. He expects us to be ready and willing to bear much fruit. This is how God gets glory out of our lives. It is using our dreams to bear more fruit that draws men unto Him. John 15:2 says,

"Every branch in me that beareth not fruit he taketh away; and every branch that beareth fruit, he purgeth it, that it may bring forth more fruit" (John 15:2).

Joseph was now ready to bring forth more fruit for the glory of God.

God disturbed Pharaoh through a dream. However, Pharaoh could not interpret the dream. In his dream, Pharaoh stood by the river Nile. Suddenly, seven well-fed cows came up out of the river and began grazing among the reeds by the bank. Then, all of a sudden, seven thin, poorly fed cows came up out of the Nile River and stood by the well feed cattle. Suddenly, the seven thin cows ate up the well-fed cows. The dream startled Pharaoh and he woke up. God disturbed Pharaoh a second time and Pharaoh awoke. Pharaoh was deeply disturbed by the dreams. He felt sure there was some significance. So, he called all the magicians and wise men to the palace. Not a single one could interpret the dreams. No one could tell Pharaoh what the dreams meant. God has the power to make men fail in meeting a need. There is every indication that God was blocking the minds of the Egyptian magicians and wise men. God was working behind the scene to work things out for His servant Joseph, and the children of Israel. Jacob and his family could not foresee the economic crisis that would devastate the land. But, God is always looking ahead into the future.

God is always working behind the scene to move us closer to our dream. He uses every event as the means to the end. God will even make the most intelligent and effective men fail, so that He will get the glory from His servants. The wisdom and power of God is infinite in helping us. **"O the depth of the riches both of wisdom and knowledge of God! How unsearchable are his judgments, and his ways past finding out! For who hath known the mind of the Lord? Or who hath been His counselor? Or who hath first given to him, and it shall be recompensed unto him again" For of him, and through him, are al things; to whom be glory for ever" (Romans 11:33-36).**

God will even make the most intelligent and effective men fail, so that He can get the glory from His servants

God stirred the chief cupbearer to remember Joseph. The cupbearer was most likely standing there watching everyone fail in interpreting the dream. Then suddenly he remembered Joseph. After two long years, the cupbearer told Pharaoh about Joseph. Joseph had interpreted the dream for the chief baker and him, and everything happened just as he said. The cupbearer suggested that Pharaoh call for Joseph. We must always remember that God causes chain of events to happen. God had already worked out things out for Joseph and His people. God can stir the mind and hearts of people to help us. We all have experienced situation where we received some unexpected help. Many times the help was from complete strangers. We must remember that these events are not accidental. Sometimes, we are helped by those who have less experience, maturity, or anointing. The hand of God orchestrates our every step. God uses people to help us get to our dream. God places people in particular places in our lives, or places us with them. Then, God uses these people to help us achieve our goals, or help us through a circumstance. In my endeavor to achieve my dreams, God has placed many people to help me. Sometimes, it was a senior executive, and other times it was the custodian, office secretary, or a church member. Each of them would encourage me to talk to certain people, or consider certain aspects of whatever I was working on. Normally, it was a causal conversation. It always seemed odd at first. Later, I realized that God was working behind the scene.

God had Joseph to be released and to stand before Pharaoh. Joseph was standing before the most powerful ruler in the world and his officers. Pharaoh came straight to the point. He told Joseph of his dreams, and that no one had been able to interpret it. Pharaoh was allowing Joseph a chance to interpret it. Joseph declared that he had no ability or power to help, but God did. Joseph said that God would help Pharaoh by giving him the meaning to his dreams. He acknowledged that only God alone could help in this situation. Joseph interpreted the dreams and was delivered from prison.

God only delivers us from our trials and circumstances after we have been properly prepared.

*We must be
prepared
to suffer
through our trials
in order to make us
a better person, and
a more diligent
steward of our
dream*

We must be prepared to suffer through our trials in order to make us a better person, and a more diligent steward of our dreams. Before your dreams can come true, God must prove you. God's process is not an easy one. When we graduate out of God's process, we are ready to meet any challenge. **"But He knoweth the way that I take; when He has tried me, I shall come forth as pure gold"** (Job 23:10).

God gave Joseph the ability to advise Pharaoh, and to show him how the need could be met. Henry Morris has an excellent description of what Pharaoh was probably thinking at this moment.

"Great trouble was ahead for the land of Egypt. As this fact began to intrude on Pharaoh's consciousness, he pondered what, if anything, he as leader of the country might be able to do about it. His people were accustomed to prosperity, with meat and bread in abundance. In fact, they provided food for export to many countries as well. How, then, would they react under famine conditions? Would they blame him? Would they lose faith in their gods? Would revolution follow?... God however, had not brought all these things to pass for the purpose of embarrassing or dethroning the king of Egypt.... The underlying purpose of it all had to do rather with God's plan for

Israel. Even Pharaoh and his great empire were like "a drop of a bucket (Isaiah 40:15) in relation to God's eternal purposes, which at this point were centered around Joseph. Therefore, not only did God give Joseph the true interpretation of the dreams, but also an effective plan of action for Pharaoh" *(The Genesis Record, p. 582.)*

Joseph recommended that Pharaoh find a qualified administrator, and put him in charge of the land of Egypt. God had created the situation for Joseph. Each step in Joseph's journey was preparing him to assume this new position. Even Joseph's recommendation to find a capable and qualified administrator was orchestrated by God. When we are ready to assume stewardship of our dreams, God will put the right words in our mouth. Remember, it is the spoken word that creates action.

"For I will give you a mouth and wisdom, which all your adversaries shall not be able to gainsay or resist" (Luke 21;15).

The advice Joseph gave was sound wisdom, and Pharaoh recognized it. Joseph also spoke with authority in his recommendation.

What happened next was a miracle! Natural man would see Joseph's transformation as a rags to riches story. Joseph was transformed from a slave to a servant, to a prisoner, and now to a ruler. The dreams that Joseph had told his family about had become a reality. Despite his suffering, he held on to his dreams. God kept His promise. Then, Pharaoh acknowledged the God of Israel. Pharaoh realized that God has revealed all this to Joseph.

And then it happened, Joseph was exalted over all the people of Egypt. Joseph was put in charge of the king's palace. Everyone except Pharaoh was subject to him. He was the second in command-over all of Egypt, over the entire land (verse 40-41). Pharaoh exalted him with the symbols of full authority. Joseph was given the ring of Pharaoh; royal linen; gold chain; and the second chariot behind Pharaoh. Pharaoh decreed that he was the first ruler, but Joseph was the second.

God has the power to bless you in marvelous ways. But, you must make yourself available to God. You must believe him, obey him, and follow him with all of your heart. God will pour His power into your life. You must continue to see yourself as chosen. You're not a dreamer, but you do have a dream. Hold on to the dreams and God will exalt you in due season. John 15:6 says,

"Ye have not chosen me, but I have chosen you, and ordained you, that ye should go and bring forth fruit, and that your fruit should remain; that whatsoever ye shall ask of the Father in my name, he may give it you" (John 15:16)

God wants you to bear fruit. The achievement of your dreams is the bearing of fruit. When God's blesses you with fruit, it remains. Your fruit will not wither away, because God gave it. Fruit is one of God's way of allowing men to see your good works that glorifies Him.   When you achieve your dream, God gets glorified, especially when you have pleaded your cause to Him. So, hold on and don't let go!

Dream Notes

- God will make even the most intelligent and effective men fail, so that He can get the glory from His servants.

- We must be prepared to suffer through our trials in order to make us a better person, and a more diligent steward of our dream

- Remember, it is the spoken word that draws our dream to us. "For I will give you a mouth and wisdom, which all your adversaries shall not be able to gainsay or resist" (Luke 21;15).

- You must continue to see yourself as chosen. You're not a dreamer, but you do have a dream.

Dream Tool

Use this dream tool to document your path to your dream. It will aid you in focusing upon what God really wants you to accomplish. Refer to this tool and use victory thinking on a monthly basis until you reach your dream. It will also help you be aligned with the will of God.

Lessons Learned
How has your suffering made you a better person?

Successes and Failures
How have you taken advantage of God positioning you in the right place?

Transition
How do you see yourself and how should you see yourself?

Seven

Now That Explains It

"But as for you, ye thought evil against me; but God meant it for good, to bring to pass, as it is this day, to save much people alive Genesis 50:20.

Joseph found favor not only in the eyes of God, but also in the eyes of men. Unfortunately, it is the eyes of God that eliminates so many from achieving their dreams. A person may have favor with men, but be a heathen in the eyes of God. We all know people that have great dreams, but they lack the morale character and love for God.   They attempt to fulfill their dreams through manipulation and shortcuts. Their only concern is to benefit themselves and their immediate circle of acquaintances.   This type of attitude falls way short of why God wants us to achieve our dreams. The bible tells us that, our success is not base upon our power or might, but God's spirit.

Joseph is listed in God's hall of fame in the eleventh chapter of Hebrews. Joseph committed himself to God, and to following the promises of God. Once he made a commitment to God, he never wavered or slipped back. He stuck to the very end. Joseph was captive in Egypt for many years. He spent almost half of his life away from his family. He had never had the opportunity to confront his brothers over the evil they had done him. Yet, Joseph had forgiven them. The famine presented Joseph with the opportunity to regain his family. Joseph showed that he had forgiven them for their evil ways. After Jacob had died, the brothers began to fear that Joseph might take vengeance against them. So, the brothers sent a message to Joseph confessing their sins, asking for forgiveness, and offering themselves as servants. Joseph would not accept their offer to be servants. He demonstrated true love and forgiveness.

> *Once you have achieved your dream, you must demonstrate true love and forgiveness.*

Once you have achieved your dreams, you must demonstrate true love and forgiveness. God was using every event along the way to prune you, and to give you a spirit of forgiveness. You can never be truly successful, unless you have the spirit of forgiveness. Hatred will make you miserable, and hinder you from enjoying your dreams. The spirit of forgiveness says once forgiven, always forgiven. The old sin or wrong is never brought up again.

"Be not overcome of evil, but overcome evil with good" (Romans 12:21).

Your commitment to follow God will make you do nothing less. You must remember that it is God's place to judge and not ours.

God devoted twelve full chapters to cover how He prepared and allowed Joseph to accomplish his dreams. Joseph endured affliction for thirty-nine years to reach his dream. However, the next fifty-four years are covered in five verses. These verses also explain why Joseph had to learn true love and forgiveness. These five verse also gives us a revelation of God's divine purpose. Why had God raised Joseph up to become second in command in Egypt? God allowed Joseph to achieve his dream for two primary reasons. These reasons may shock you. One would think that Joseph was being rewarded for enduring the suffering and hardship, while being held captive in Egypt. We could also theorize that God was demonstrating that good would always overcome evil. However God allowed Joseph to reach his true potential in the will of God, so that

- He could help save the land of Egypt from total economical collapse and starvation during the seven-year famine.

- He could bring Israel down to Egypt to facilitate fulfilling his promise to Abraham. Also, to save them from the worldly influence and intermarriage with the Canaanites.

After you have become successful, it would be easy to forget about the salvation of others. It would be easy to forget that God has given us His benefits for the achievement of good. So, why does God allow us to achieve our dreams. **Reaching our dreams is really about God and His salvation.** Genesis chapter 50 verse 20 really explains it. We are one chess piece in

God's game of chess. Just like in chess, God is working to get us to kingship and win the game. He allows us to have successes and benefits to continue to further His Kingdom. We reap the benefits, but God gets the complete glory. God will keep his promise, and afford us the best that heaven has to give. But, His determination is that every man might be saved. We must not think of our dream achievement in a selfish way. We have to think of it as a larger purpose. God is attempting to save much

Reaching our dreams is really about God and His plan of salvation.

people alive. God wants to use us, and our ability along with His investment of experiences to help deliver others. God will allow us to enjoy great benefits, as a reward. God will grant us peace, riches , and honor for the remainder of our life. However, God wants everyone saved.

Joseph achieved his dream, so that God could save the entire Egyptian world from financial collapse. Joseph's true love for people and forgiveness of his brothers permitted him to accomplish both of God's purposes. God had overruled evil and worked it out for good. God had used Joseph to save the world, but especially His people, Israel, the believers of the earth. Joseph declared that he must repay evil with good. Joseph's declaration should define our nature. We must overcome evil by using the good that comes out of achieving our dreams.

We must overcome evil by using the good that comes out of achieving our dream.

How did Joseph live the rest of his life" Joseph remained faithful to God. God had completed His primary purpose for Joseph by the time Joseph was fifty-six years old. He worked to keep his brothers together. He lived a godly and righteous life before the world of his day. Joseph was faithful to the end. Joseph was not only faithful, but also fruitful.

The result was a wonderful blessing from God; God was giving fruit to Joseph; grandchildren who were to become the future believers of God upon the earth. Even in Joseph's grandchildren, God received the glory.

Joseph held on to his dreams into death. When he was 110 years of age, he faced death. As he was dying, Joseph wanted his brethren to know that the promises of God are true. God was going to keep them through all of their afflictions, and eventually God was going to take them to the Promised Land Even in his death, Joseph demonstrated his faith by demanding an oath from his brothers. He made them swear to carry his bones back to the promised land when they returned. This was one of the greatest declaration of faith in the promise of God.

This is an example of the ultimate sign of holding on to a dreams. No matter how long it would be, Joseph wanted to declare his faith in the most significant way he could. Throughout his life, he had given a strong witness to God, In death, Joseph wanted the same testimony. He wanted to declare even with his bones, that God makes dreams come true.

Dream Notes

- Once you have achieved your dream, you must demonstrate true love and forgiveness.

- Reaching our dreams is really about God and His salvation

- We must overcome evil by using the good that comes out of achieving our dream.

Dream Tool

Use this dream tool to document your path to your dream. It will aid you in focusing upon what God really wants you to accomplish. Refer to this tool and use victory thinking on a monthly basis until you reach your dream. It will also help you be aligned with the will of God.

Lessons Learned
What have you learned about commitment and following God?

Successes and Failures
How have your failures allowed you to demonstrate faith in God?

Transition
What is God doing to prepare you for your next steps?

Eight

A Certain Place for a Certain Reason

"And Joseph said unto his brethren, I die; and God will surely visit you, and bring you out of this land unto the land which He swore to Abraham, to Isaac, and to Jacob.

Your reading this little book is not an accident. It is by divine providence. I believe that God places us in certain places for certain reasons. Perhaps, this is your appointment with destiny. Or perhaps, God wants you to share this little book with someone struggling with his or her dreams. Either way, God is letting you know that He wants you to reach your full potential in His will. Sometimes, our full potential is only realized through the testing of our faith. So, God places us in certain places that will help us overcome our fears. His reason is to always work a blessing through us. In all cases, God is working a larger plan. We are only the conduits that He works through.

Joseph was taken captive, so that he could be delivered to the place that would provide salvation for his family. However, Joseph being taken to Egypt was only part of a larger plan. God had maneuvered him to Egypt for even a greater purpose. God's reason was revealed to Joseph's Great grandfather Abraham.

Genesis 15: 13 –14 verse outlines God's plan for Israel.

"And He said unto Abram, Know of a surety that thy seed shall be a stranger on a land that is not theirs, and shall serve them; and they shall afflict them four hundred years; and also that nation, whom they shall serve, will I judge; and afterward shall they come out with great substance"

God ultimate plan for Joseph arriving in Egypt was to make Israel a great nation. God prophesied that the children of Israel would be in bondage for 400 years, but would come out with great substance. In other words, God would let them remain captive for 400 years. When Israel left Egypt, they were rich. Not just a few were rich, but the whole nation was rich. God placed Joseph in Egypt, so that the children of Israel would grow in size and ultimately leave Egypt with wealth that they would take to the promise land.

There is a certain place that God has assigned for you. God cannot work out the next steps in your destiny, until you arrive in that certain place. Have you ever wondered why you were inspired or motivated to leave your hometown, a job, or even a church? When you were quizzed, or even challenged, you had no good reason. Even if you had a reason, it wasn't a concrete one. It is simply because God want you in that certain place. The reason may not be clear. However, you must have real faith that God is working all things together for you. The scriptures are full of examples. Accepting the your present status is key to achieving your dreams. We cannot complain or murmur. Murmuring and complaining hinders our progress. We must accept the certain place as part of our destiny.

God has placed me in some unusual places in my life. At one time in my life, I question everything that God was doing. I often asked God why this or that was happening. Why was I in this challenge or crisis? One day God responded with why not. God has no respecter of person. God is just using us to accomplish His divine will. In the process, we receive blessings press down, shaken together, and running over. More importantly, accepting our certain place puts us in position to receive our inheritance.

When you find yourself in certain places of challenges, you should rejoice. It is a demonstration that you have favor with God. You should not think that it is the devil. The devil cannot accomplish anything more than what God allows. You should not think your certain place is because of some sin. Romans 8:1 says,

"There is therefore now no more condemnation to them which are in Christ, who walk not after the flesh; but after the Spirit"

Your current surroundings, relationships, church membership, job, and economic status are for a certain reason. God is attempting to accomplish something through you. God wants you to accomplish your dreams. This is how He accomplished His divine will.

Nine

Make Your Dream Come True

The story of Joseph's life is rich with revelations of how God works in our lives. How God inspires us with dreams, and then works to help make the dream come true. This book is not about dreaming, but about your dreams. That one thing or things that God has placed in your spirit to bless you, and help others fulfill their true potential in the will of God.

I want to encourage you to use the principles contained in this book to help you get a greater revelation of your destiny. Use this book as a roadmap to understand how and what God is doing through you. God is a God of order, so you can be assured that these steps will come to pass.

For the best results, I recommend that you do the following

1. Write out your dreams and tape it in your Bible, day-timer, or some other place where you can stay reminded of your destiny.

2. Reread this little book once per quarter, asking God to give you revelations of His will for your life. Use the Dream Tool Guide at the end of each chapter to help you in obtaining your

revelation. The Dream Tool Guide will provide guideposts to keep you focused and on target.

3. Reread the Dream Notes on a regular basis. The Dream notes will help to encourage you, as you walk through each step to your destiny.

4. Begin to keep a diary of major events in your life. Write your daily events each day. It will provide a clearer view of how God is allowing all things to work together for your good.

5. Share your success from reading this little book with others. It is not until we show true love, forgiveness, and humility that God unleashes His mighty power in our lives.

Obviously, the Bible contains many stories, scriptures, and prayers that can unleash the favor of God upon your life. Like many other books, this book is an attempt to share with you insights based on my experiences, and how I have seen God work with others over the last twenty years of being a Pastor and a Senior Executive. God has allowed me to accomplish my early dreams. Now, God has set me on a new course for even greater dreams for His glory.

As you read this book, my prayer is that you not be just a reader of the word, but a doer also.

About the Author

Bishop J.C. Parks accepted his ministerial calling on February 6, 1976. He has a rich background in pastoral and academic achievement. He has been a pastor since the age of 19, and is presently pastor of the New Hope Missionary Baptist church of Winston Salem, North Carolina. During his ten years at New Hope, a new church has been built, and has experienced tremendous growth. A second expansion is planned for December 2002. Bishop Parks has been anointed, appointed, and approved to preach and teach to this present age. He has conducted revivals, conferences, and workshops throughout the South East United States. In July 2002, Pastor Parks made history by becoming the first Baptist to be consecrated Bishop by the Pentecostal denomination.

Bishop Parks is also a senior Executive of a major Fortune 500 company. He was the first African American to achieve this position. He has managed business organizations exceeding 1,000 employees. He also has over twenty years in managerial experience. He participates on many Executive Boards and is heavily involved in economical and educational enrichment for the poor.

Bishop Parks received an Electrical Engineering degree from Tennessee State University of Nashville Tennessee, a Masters of Business from Wake Forest University of Winston Salem, North Carolina, and a certificate of Executive studies from Stanford University.

More Resources to Help Your Spiritual Growth

Coming Soon

Dream Chasers.

A weekly devotional, instructional guide, and Dream Tools designed to help you continue receiving revelations from God. Dream Nuggets is intended to aid you in your spiritual development and accomplishment of all of your goals and dreams.

Begin Again

We all make some judgments and have failures that hinder our success in life. These setbacks can become strong holds that prevent God from completing His perfect work in you. This book will help you pull down the strongholds that are interfering with your destiny. The secret to success is knowing how to begin again.